CONTENTS

D1114001

Chongqing Province, China
Photograph by Edward Jung

INTRODUCTION

Ping pong is the most popular racquet sport in the world, the second most popular participation sport in the world after football, and the most popular sport in China bar none. Yet somehow, despite the many millions of people who are playing the game as you read this, ping pong has retained an atmosphere of sub-culture. Of a sport that has somehow crept out of the basement and into the public eye. Suddenly ping pong is not just popular, it's also cool. Tables are popping up in outdoor spaces and hipster bars all over the world. The health benefits are being applauded by neuroscientists who say that ping pong is the number one brain sport, increasing IQ, fending off dementia and boosting virility (ok maybe not that one). Celebrities are jumping on the bandwagon, with people like Susan Sarandon picking up their bats and opening clubs from Manhattan to Milwaukee. Yes indeed, ping pong is out and it's proud.

So what are the allures of the game? Well, beyond that deeply satisfying pop-popping sound that is in itself a tonic for the soul, ping pong is one of very few sports that is truly democratic. Gender, race, nationality, age and physique have no real bearing on how well you can play. It's a game that's enjoyable at all levels, but that has endless room for improvement. As a result, it has a friendly, inclusive, sociable quality that is a rare find in the sporting arena. Finally, there is a thrill to ping pong that is hard to put your finger on. It's fast and it's unpredictable. Sometimes, when you tap that dinky little ball, it flicks off your bat in a completely unexpected way – and all of a sudden you've beaten a player that you never expected to beat. And that crazy rush you get – it keeps you coming back for more.

This book is an introduction to the sport of ping pong. It will guide you through some basic rules and techniques to improve your game, but it is also a survey of the culture surrounding the game; the design, the aesthetics and the venues that are emerging to cater to the sport's hip new image. Because whether you're a geek or a god, a novice or a pro, it's always worth playing the game with style.

THE EQUIPMENT

THE TABLE

The table must measure 2.74m x 1.525m. It should be 76cm off the floor, with a net that is 15.25cm high, spanning the entire table (and in professional games, it should extend 15.25cm beyond the end of the table at either end).

38 mm

The paddle can be of any size and weight. You can use your iPhone, a book or a pizza box. However, one side must be red and the other black. If you are buying a paddle, look for one with a smooth rubber surface, rather than a pimpled texture. This is better for spin.

THE BALL

The ball should measure 38mm in diameter and can be either orange or white. Buy good balls, cheap balls crack and are less fun.

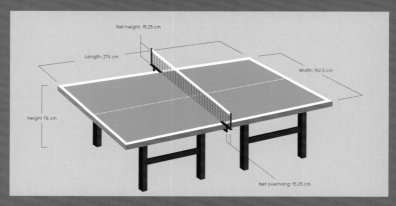

Net height: 15.25 cm

Length: 274 cm

Width: 152.5 cm

Height 76 cm

Net overhang: 15.25 cm

THE GRIP

SHAKEHANDS GRIP is the standard grip in Western countries.

PEN GRIP is favoured by many Asian players. It limits your range, but gives you very fine control. Experiment with both.

Beijing
Photograph by Foxxyz

THE RULES

- A game of ping pong is played up to 11 points. It used to be up to 21, but the rules changed in 2001. A match is usually the best of five games.

- First you need to decide who serves. The most common method is to hide the ball in one hand, then put both hands behind your back or under the table and ask your opponent to guess which one it's in. Alternatively you can toss a coin.

- When serving, the ball is hit so that it bounces first on the server's side and then at least once on the opponent's side of the table.

- The players get two serves each, alternating until one player scores 11 points. Players must win by two points. If both players score ten points (deuce), the service then alternates after each point until one player wins by two points.

- When receiving the ball, the player must hit it after it has bounced once on their side of the table. Players cannot hit the ball before it has bounced on their side.

- Players change ends after each game. The player who served first in the previous game receives first in the next.

10

A PLAYER
SCORES WHEN

- Their opponent fails to make a good service.

- Their opponent fails to make a good return.

- Their opponent obstructs the ball in play – i.e. they, or anything they wear or carry, touches the ball when it is in flight.

- Their opponent moves the playing surface (eg. shifting the table when lunging for the ball).

- Their opponent's hand touches the playing surface.

Nepal
Photograph by
Marcin Rozpedowski

12

DOUBLES RULES

- In doubles the rules are the same except that the table is divided in two lengthwise. The ball must first hit the server's quadrant of the table and then bounce at least one in the diagonal quadrant facing the receiver.

- The order of play is key to doubles ping pong. The players from each team take turns returning shots, so that the order of the game follows a clear structure: If we have two teams – A&B and C&D – the order would go: **A > C > B > D**

- At each change of service, the previous receiver (C) becomes the server, and the partner of the previous server becomes the receiver (B). So the next game would follow the order: **C > B > D > A**

- Once it has been decided which team serves first, that team can then decide which player serves first (A or B). Their opponents will then decide which player in their team receives first (C or D). In the next game, C and D will decide who serves first, but A and B's roles will automatically be determined by reversing the sequence of the previous game.

- After every game, the players must switch ends of the table. However, in a game that has the potential to be the last game of the match, the teams switch ends again once a team has scored five points, and also, the receiving pair must change their order of receiving. So if you're playing a best-of-five match, and team A has won the first two matches, you will swap sides halfway through the third match. If team B wins that match, you'll swap sides again at the start of game four, and again once five points have been scored.

Photograph by Garry Maclennan
www.garrymaclennan.com

THE SERVE

The serve is the most important shot in ping pong – but is often overlooked by junior players, who focus more on their rally techniques. The serve is the only shot where you have complete control of the ball, and if you set it up properly, gives you a substantial advantage in the ensuing rally. The rules of serving are as follows:

- Standing behind the end of the table, the server holds the ball in the flat palm of their non-playing hand, above the level of the table, and throws it upwards. The ball can't be hidden from the opponent at any point, and must not have any spin on it as it is thrown.

- As the ball falls downwards, the server hits the ball with their bat, so that it bounces once on their side of the table and at least once on the opponent's side.

- If the ball hits the net, but continues to the opponent's side, the server retakes the serve. If the ball doesn't make it to the other side, the server loses the point.

Deception has always been an important part of serving. This is your chance to catch your opponent on the back-foot, and assert your control over the rally. Your degree of deception is limited by the way you have to present the ball, but there are ways and means of trickery that you should master.

SPIN

Whilst you can't put spin on the toss, you can impart spin on the ball when you hit it. By brushing your paddle up or down against the ball, you change the nature of the shot (see pp. 27–29).

LENGTH OF SERVE

A **SHORT SERVE** is most effective. What this means is that the ball hits your side about halfway to the net, and has the potential to bounce twice on the opponent's side with the second bounce being on the baseline. This shot requires your opponent to lean over the table, limiting the power of their return, and leaving them less time to recover for your next shot.

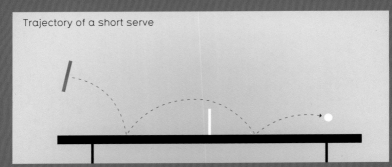

Trajectory of a short serve

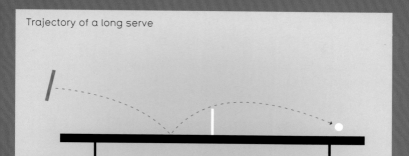

Trajectory of a long serve

A **LONG SERVE** bounces once towards the edge of your opponent's side and is faster. If you catch your opponent off-guard it's great, but if not, you might be setting yourself up for a strong return. Aim for the deep corners. Any shot that chips the edge of the table will be virtually impossible to return.

BALL HEIGHT

Throwing the ball higher translates to more speed, but can be harder to control. Higher level players aim to hit the ball as low as possible – about 20cm above the table. Experiment with different ball-heights, and be careful not to allow your opponent to guess what serve you are using from the height of the toss.

TIPS

- Mix up serves with different length and spin. Keep your opponent guessing.
- Use your serve to set up your next shot, rather than using it as a killer shot every time.
- Experiment with different serves and try them out early on in the match. Work out what's most effective and adjust your tactics accordingly.

New Ulm, Minnesota, 1979
Photograph by Paul Dagys

Bonn, Germany
Photograph by Ninette

Photograph by Garry Maclennan
www.garrymaclennan.com

THE SPIN

Spin is your friend. Understanding how to put spin on a ball, and how to counter the spin that's put on a ball by your opponent is the one thing that will truly transform your game. Combining different types of spin with different types of shot is what the game is all about.

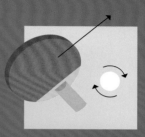

TOPSPIN

In topspin the bat is angled downwards (a 'closed bat') and meets the ball with an upward slice. The result is that the ball spins in the direction of the stroke, flies fast, and shoots forward after the bounce. The height of the bounce depends on where the bat makes contact with the ball. Topspin is the most important technique to master.

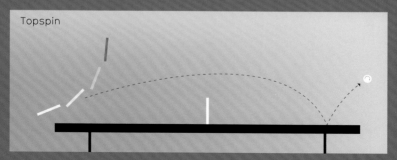

Topspin

BACKSPIN

In backspin, the bat is angled backwards (an 'open bat'), and meets the ball with a downward chop. This results in a ball that is spinning against the direction of the stroke, leading to a slower shot that loses speed after the bounce. This means that it is more likely to bounce close to your opponent's side of the net, causing them to have to lunge for the ball.

SIDESPIN

This stroke is usually used in combination with topspin or backspin. Rather than playing the spin straight on the ball, you hit the ball slightly to one side or the other. If combined with topspin, the shot will veer in the direction played. With backspin, it will veer in the opposite direction.

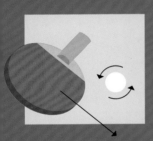

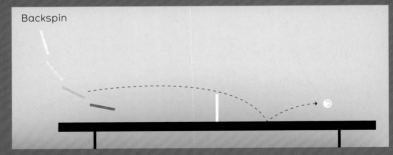

Backspin

Sayid Abad, Afghanistan
Photograph by Chase Steely

TIP

Learn to recognise the type of spin your opponent is putting on the ball, so that you can respond accordingly. This will only really come with time, but a good place to start is practicing your own shots in front of the mirror. Look at your stance and the angle of the bat for each shot. Use the logo on the ball as a point of reference.

KEY STROKES

There are so many strokes you could learn in ping pong, but you're best to start off with the drives and pushes.

THE DRIVES

Drives are your main form of offense. They usually impart a light topspin, and are easy for beginners to master.

FOREHAND DRIVE

- Stand with your feet facing the table and your bat held close to you, but not flush to you, at hip height.

- Hit the ball at the top of the bounce. Swing your bat up and forward, finishing with your hand just above shoulder height around the mid-line of your body.

- Let your waist turn with the shot, shifting your weight to the other foot as you move.

- Limit your wrist action. The movement should mostly come from your forearm, with your elbow as the pivot point.

BACKHAND DRIVE

Slightly trickier to master, this is a shorter, faster shot than the forehand drive, well worth investing in.

- Stand close to the table and face exactly where you want the ball to go.

- Hold the bat across your body with your elbow at a 90 degree angle, close to, but not touching, your stomach.

- The face of the bat should be angled down towards the table.

- Try to hit the ball at the top of the bounce. Snap the forearm with a slightly upwards movement. The power comes from the forearm and wrist.

- Strike the ball with power, and follow through so that your paddle ends up pointing in the direction of the shot. Final speed can be added by flicking the wrist at the last moment.

TIP
If you return diagonally, you have
more room for your shot and are less
likely to miss the table.

THE PUSHES

Push strokes are defensive plays, great for countering backspin and slower shots. They should be played lightly, unlike the drives, and ideally you want to impart a little backspin of your own.

FOREHAND PUSH

- Start with your bat beside you at hip height, tilted slightly towards the ceiling.

- Swing down and forwards, lightly hitting the bottom half of the ball immediately after the bounce.

- Finish with your bat near the table and your palm facing the ceiling.

- Try to keep your swing short. This will keep the ball nice and low over the net, and will prevent your opponent from getting in a strong return

BACKHAND PUSH

- Start with the bat close to your stomach, palm facing towards you and the face slightly tilted back towards the ceiling. The more spin your opponent has played, the more your bat should be tilted.

- Swing down and forward, lightly grazing the bottom of the ball, and finish with your palm facing the table.

- Once again, the shorter your swing, the lower and slower the ball, making it harder for your opponent to return.

Photograph by Garry Maclennan
www.garrymaclennan.com

THE BLOCK

The block shot is a kind of abbreviated drive that is a useful tool against a powerful topspin shot. Short and sharp, it allows you to use your opponent's force against them, catching them out of position. Backhand and forehand blocks use similar techniques:

- Stand close to the table facing the direction that you want the ball to go.

- Just after the ball bounces, hit it using a short stroke, moving your arm from the elbow in a horizontal plane. Don't follow through. It's a quick snap shot with minimal body movement.

- The bat is played closed to neutralise your opponent's spin. The more spin on the ball, the more closed the racket should be.

- Use your wrist to angle the return towards your opponent's baseline or side-line.

THE SMASH

The smash is the hardest drive you can play. Spin is of less importance than power. It's mostly used to return a shot that your opponent has hit high.

When the ball is at the top of its bounce, throw your whole body behind the bat, and slam it down so that the ball goes fast enough to be unreturnable.

It's a trickier shot than it looks and can veer out of control quite easily. Make sure to get the angle of the bat right, keeping an open bat against backspin and a closed one against topspin.

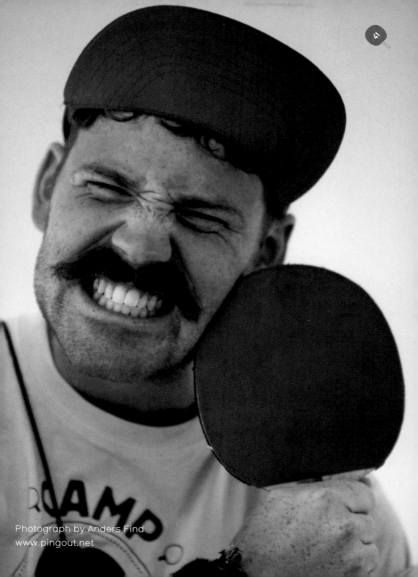

Photograph by Sean Marc Lee

PRACTICE ON YOUR OWN

There are a few ways to practice on your own without an opponent.

- For beginners, the playback option can be helpful. Adjust the table so that one half of it is in a vertical position, serving as a backboard. This is a good way to build up fast responses and practice some basic shots. However, the angles of return, the speed and the variation of spin are not in any way reflective of an opponent, and can result in bad habits.

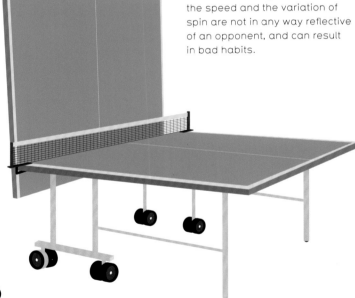

- More advanced players should practice shadow play: Stand in front of a mirror and practice your shots without a ball. Make sure to pay attention to stance.

- Practice your footwork. Particularly shuffle stepping, which is your main way of moving across the court. Sashay from side to side. Your left foot should be 20cm or so closer to the court than your right at all times (or the other way around if you are left-handed).

- Practice your serve. Over and over. Repeat the same serve until you get it right. Aim at targets on the table, so you can get a precise shot. Don't ever hold more than one ball in your hand when you're practicing a serve, as the throw will be distorted.

- Practice your spin by hitting a ball on the floor and seeing how you can make it come back to you or make it curve away.

- Bounce the ball on the bat to increase ball control.

- Look on YouTube for footage of professional matches and for shot specific tutorials. Watch and learn.

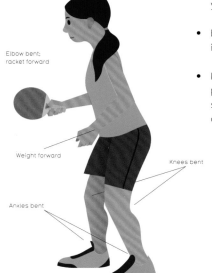

Elbow bent; racket forward

Weight forward

Knees bent

Ankles bent

The ready position

PING PONG
IN DESIGN

Ping Pong equipment is pretty
basic. A table, two bats and a ball.
And yet the culture and aesthetic
surrounding the game have
provided creative inspiration to
numerous exciting designers. These
are a few favourites. They might not
all meet International Table Tennis
Federation standards, but they
capture that alternative, subversive
element that makes ping pong so
unequivocally cool.

Kelli Mink Paddle Case

Pam Schriever

www.pamschriever.com

James de Wulf

www.jamesdewulf.com

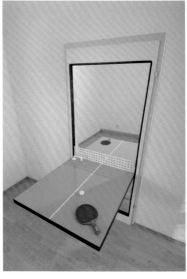

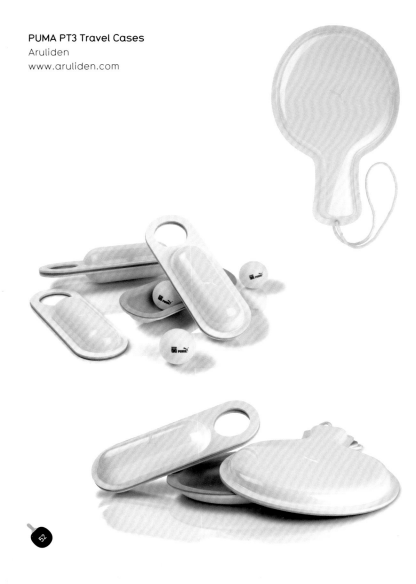

PUMA PT3 Travel Cases
Aruliden
www.aruliden.com

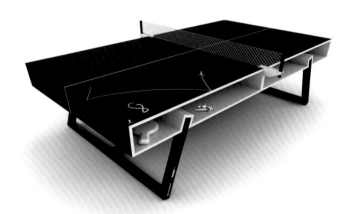

Ping Pong Cover for iPhone
Incase
www.goincase.com

King Pong Table
Billi Kid
www.billikid.com

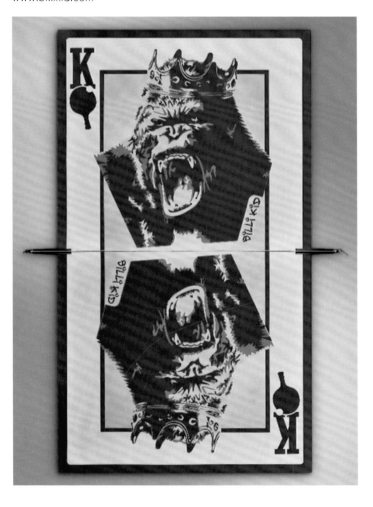

FOUR OTHER GAMES TO PLAY WITH A PING PONG BALL

BEER PONG

There are a multitude of drinking related ping pong games (and hey, all games can be drinking related if you want them to be), but the most famous is beer pong. Rules vary, but the traditional format is to place six or ten cups full of beer in pyramid formation at both ends of a big table. The players are then divided into two teams (usually of two or four players), and each team shoots ping pong balls into their opponents' cups. When a ball lands in a cup, that team must consume the contents of it, and replace it in the pyramid. If the opposite team throws a ping pong ball into an empty cup, they have to consume one of their own cups. The last team with any beer-filled cups left wins.

CIVIL WAR

Along the same lines as beer pong. Two teams of two players stand at either side of the table with four cups of beer in front of each one. They then try to throw balls in the opposing team's cups, while shielding their own. There are no turns, it's just a free-for-all. If a ball lands in your cup, you must stop playing until you've drunk the contents. Your teammate defends your cups while you are thus occupied. The team with no beer left loses.

SQUIRT BALL

Fill three two-litre soda bottles halfway with water, and set a ping pong ball on the top of each bottle. Take a squirt bottle (or water pistol), and try to spray the balls off the soda bottles.

PING PONG BOWLING

Set up dominos in a ten-pin bowling formation spaced around four centimetres from each other. Roll a ping pong ball and try to knock them down.

Poughkeepsie
Photograph by John Mehrkens
Edited by Chris Melberger

PING PONG
BARS AROUND
THE WORLD

LONDON

The Book Club 100-106 Leonard St, London EC2A 4RH; www.wearetbc. com; *This Shoreditch hang-out has a dedicated ping pong room and holds a King Pong singles knockout tournament every Tuesday night.*

Doodle Bar 33 Parkgate Rd, London SW11 4NP; *Fun ping pong bar in an old Battersea warehouse.*

BRISTOL

Ping Pong Parlour Unit 15, Princess St, Bristol BS2 0RA; *A friendly social club and bar with good music and eight tables.*

BRIGHTON

The Latest Music Bar 14-16 Manchester St, Brighton, BN2 1TF; *A monthly ping pong event in this great party venue.*

LOS ANGELES

Round One Puente Hills Mall, 1600 S Azusa Ave, Ste 285, City of Industry, CA 91748; www.round1usa.com; *Classic arcade games, Japanese photo booths, a bowling alley, karaoke rooms and ping pong tables.*

Prince O' Whales 335 Culver Blvd, Playa Del Rey, CA 90293; www. princeowhales.com; *Dive bar with mellow down-home vibe and a ping pong patio with three tables.*

SAN FRANCISCO

Thee Parkside 1600 17th St, San Francisco, CA 94107; www. theeparkside.com; *Dark, dirty with ping pong tables on a covered patio. A rec room for grown-ups.*

NEW YORK

Fat Cat 75 Christopher St, New York, NY 10014; www.fatcatmusic.org; *Bar. Live jazz. Ping Pong. Awesome.*

Spin NYC 48 E 23rd St, New York, NY 10010; www.spingalactic.com; *Opened in 2009 by Susan Sarandon, this is now a chain with branches in Milwaukee and Toronto. Exclusively dedicated to ping pong, it has coaches, beer and everything else a true enthusiast could desire.*

Iona 180 Grand St, Brooklyn, NY 11211; www.ionabrooklyn.com; *Large, fun bar behind Grand Street Bus Station in Williamsburg.*

WASHINGTON DC

Comet Ping Pong 5037 Connecticut Ave NW, Washington DC 20008; *Cool décor, great pizza, buzzing atmosphere.*

NEW ORLEANS

Shamrock 4133 S Carrollton Ave, New Orleans, LA 70119; www.shamrockparty.com; *Eight dartboards, 23 pool tables, a million TVs, five enclosed ping pong tables.*

TORONTO

Spin 461 King St West, Toronto, ON M5V 1K7; *14 tables and good food.*

SYDNEY

Gaffa Gallery 281 Clarence St, Sydney, NSW 2000; www.gaffa.com.au; *Three storeys of galleries, great coffee and free ping pong.*

BERLIN

Dr Pong Eberswalder Str 21, Prenzlauer Berg, Berlin; www.drpong.net; *All night ping pong. And beer.*

AMSTERDAM

OT301 Vereniging Eerst Hulp Bij Kunst, Overtoom 301, 1054 HW Amsterdam; www.ot301.nl; *An alternative cultural centre and club.*

MADRID

Matadero de Madrid Matadero de Legazpi, Paseo de la Chopera 10, 28045 Madrid; www.mataderomadrid.org; *A slaughterhouse turned arts centre with cinemas, design spaces, bars and ping pong tables.*

STOCKHOLM

Bar Brooklyn Hornstull Strand 4, 117 39 Stockholm; *Great bar where you can get up to 30 people participating in a rally ping pong tournament.*

MOSCOW

Denis Simachev Bar Stoleshnikov pereulok 12,bldg 2, Moscow; *High end fashionista bar with table.*

TOKYO

Nakame Takkyu Lounge Line-house Nakameguro 2F 1-3-13 Kamimeguro, Meguro-ku; *An underground ping pong bar hidden inside an apartment block.*

Berry 3F Fujiya Bldg, 1-3-9 Kamimeguro, Meguro-ku, Tokyo; www.justanotherspace.com; *Another Nakameguro speakeasy hidden in an industrial complex.*

Top: Doodle Bar, London;
Bottom: Spin, New York

Published by Cicada Books Limited

Written and edited by Ziggy Hanaor
Design by April
Illustration by Seif Alhassani

British Library Cataloguing-in-Publication Data
A CIP record for this book is available from the
British Library
ISBN: 978-1-908714-01-5

Many thanks to all the photographers and
models who contributed material to this
book. Especially Garry Maclennan (www.
garrymaclennan.co.uk) for his awesome
photoshoot. Thanks to The Book Club in
London for letting us use their space. Finally,
big thanks to Jamie Chan for her advice,
input and general classiness.

Printed in China

Cicada Books Limited
48 Burghley Road
London, NW5 1UE

E: ziggy@cicadabooks.co.uk
W: www.cicadabooks.co.uk